Burnarounds:

Unlocking The Double Digit Profit Code

Transforming the small company
into a Global Powerhouse

Steven L. Blue

Burnarounds: Unlocking The Double Digit Profit Code
Transforming The Small Company Into A Global Powerhouse
All Rights Reserved.
Copyright © 2009 Steven L. Blue
V3.0

Editing and formatting by Your Writing Partner,
www.YourWritingPartner.net
Cover design by Killercovers.com

ISBN: 978-1-60725-252-8

For more information or to purchase additional copies,
Contact
Steven L. Blue
78 Shady Oak Ct.
Winona, MN 55987
steve@burnarounds.com

PRINTED IN THE UNITED STATES OF AMERICA

What Readers Are Saying

Cutting to the chase as though there were no tomorrow (and for many businesses there might not be), Steve Blue presents startling and enlightening imperatives of business survival and transformation, perfectly suited for these challenging times. This is a "do it" book ... do it or die ... simple as that. His message will instruct and inspire every good leader.

Bud Baechler, Entrepreneur and Business Advisor

Steve Blue shows how to value time as a currency equal to money, with zero tolerance for mediocrity in people and performance. I've seen him walk the talk in quickly lopping off those who refuse to get with the program, but celebrating those who do, with the results showing up in the financial statements. You can follow his simple (but not easy) lessons... if you have the courage.

Norm Stoehr, Founder Inner Circle
International Ltd.

Steve Blue provides a framework to maximize firm efficiency in a global economy. He promotes an aggressive approach to whip underperforming companies into shape. His straightforward, no-nonsense blueprint provides an easy-to-follow guide to transforming an organization by addressing hard issues that many companies would rather avoid.

Dr. Greg Filbeck, CFA, FRM, CAIA
Professor of Finance, Penn State Behrend

In his hard-hitting and direct book, *Burnarounds*, Steve Blue slaps readers out of their slumber and shows leaders how they can take control back into their own hands. He shows direct and proven ways to boost company performance from ho-hum to "wow." *Burnarounds* is much more than a cookbook—it's a blueprint for supercharging your sleeping giant of a company into an organization that is profitable and a great place to work for all. I recommend this book for any leader with guts enough to stage their own *burnaround* (you'll never regret it).

James D. Kestenbaum, PhD, The Solutions Group

This book is a fast-paced and efficient read for today's busy executives and business owners. Steve masterfully blends personal career experiences with real-world examples to illustrate key aspects of the *Burnaround* strategy. Any company with an exportable product should definitely heed Steve's advice and begin selling overseas in order to increase profits!

Stephen Woessner, Business Education Outreach
Coordinator, Small Business Development Center
University of Wisconsin-La Crosse

About the Author

Steve Blue's mantra is "double sales and triple profits." He knows how to transform any small company into a global powerhouse. He knows how to transform single-digit earnings into 20%+ operating profit. Time and time again he finds trapped value in any business and unleashes it, resulting in explosive growth in sales and profits. He has extensive experience in forming and growing highly profitable international relationships that allow a small company to do business like a huge one.

Steve is the president and CEO of a privately-held multinational manufacturer of products for the worldwide transportation industry. He doubled sales and tripled profit without any infusion of outside capital, all the while increasing shareholder distributions. Steve calls it the "pay as you grow" system.

Before joining his current company, Steve headed the global products business of a unit of Sasib S.p.a., a large international conglomerate, where he increased sales by 34% and profit by 56%. His division introduced more products in two years than the rest of the company did in decades.

He has also held a variety of senior management positions with Fortune 500 companies, including General Signal and Rockwell International.

Steve is a published author of trade magazine articles on management and has been a guest lecturer at the Harvard Business School. He holds a BS degree from the State University of New York and an MBA from Regis University.

Table of Contents

Introduction to *Burnarounds*

Most small companies languish in single-digit earnings as a percent of sales. When I ask them why they aren't earning double digits, they excuse their performance with statements like, "We perform on a level with our peers" or "We are right on track with the average profits in our industry."

These companies are anemic and don't even know it. They are in the middle of a slowly developing crisis that will engulf them in the coming global war of the business worlds. Worse, they are headed for a turnaround (a company that needs to change direction and drastically and quickly improve its profit to keep from going out of business) and don't know *that* either! By the time they know they need a turnaround, it will probably be too late. If they come out on the other side at all, they won't ever be the same.

"That's not my company," you say. No? Let's find out. The symptoms of a company headed for

> Everyone was doing their jobs when the Titanic went down!

oblivion are clear and unmistakable. Before you waste your money buying this book, let's see if your company has any of the symptoms.

Do your senior managers play the "I can't control game"? You know what I mean: Sales can't control when Manufacturing constructs the product. Manufacturing can't control the promises Sales makes. Product Development can't control what Manufacturing does. I'll bet your whole company plays this game. And you want to know the worst part? You go along with it. Sound familiar?

Speaking of your senior managers, whose team do they play on? Your sales executives probably play solely on the sales team. Your manufacturing people play on the manufacturing team. Quality owes its allegiance to the quality function. Everybody doing their jobs, right? Don't forget, everyone was doing their jobs when the Titanic went down too.

What about Manufacturing? Is your cost-of-sales going down significantly every single year? Or do you buy into the "we can't do anything about costs" argument? Hmm, I thought so.

Is every person in your company a superstar, soon to be a hotshot, or soon to be an ex-employee? Do your human-resources people tell you this scenario is not practicable?

Let's try something a little easier. Who's responsible for profit in your company? If you are the CEO, are you the only one responsible?

Or is everyone accountable for profit?

Your salespeople work for the customer, not your company, right? Do you buy the sales argument that "the customer pays the bills"?

Does it appear that things just don't seem to get done in your company? Do you hear an endless string of reasons why more progress isn't made? Does there seem to be a lot of activity but few results?

Does your company have a culture that you have chosen? Or is it a culture by default? Is the culture profit-oriented, accountability-focused, passionate and committed?

If your company doesn't have these symptoms, don't bother reading this book. But I'll bet you have most of them.

Want to know how I know that? Because these are the symptoms of most single-digit-earnings (as a percent of sales) companies. This is the world you probably live in, unless you are running an oil company or a pharmaceutical company. Earnings in the single digits are the exception, rather than the rule, in most businesses.

It doesn't have to be that way. I know. I have taken small, Rustbelt, low-technology businesses and transformed them into double-digit-earning global powerhouses. And I am talking 20+% earnings as a percent of sales.

I have built teams that launched blizzards of industry-first products. Changed cultures from worst-in-class to best-in-breed. Created global alliances from vaporware. And you can too.

I learned how to do this the hard way. I lived through the worst management nightmare you can imagine in a turnaround: deciding whether to pay the electricity bill or payroll, caught between militant unions and unreasonable absentee foreign shareholders, negotiating unlikely-to-succeed deals. I had bricks thrown through my living room window and was forced to agree to unjustifiable objectives just to make the boss look good. I attended 16-hour marathon meetings, day after day, where nothing was done but pass the blame—using any excuse we could think of just to get out of the room alive. Despite that, I created a winning team that was the envy of the industry. Just another day in the life of a turnaround!

I also learned how to do this the fun way: taking terrific businesses and making them spectacular, creating unheard of sales-per-employee numbers, doubling sales and tripling profit. Just another day in the life of a company that *acts* like it needs a turnaround. It was with these experiences that I discovered the path to the elite world of double-digit earnings: the *Burnaround*.

A *Burnaround* combines the best features of a turnaround and a successful company. It results in an awesome combination that ignites lackluster companies and great companies alike to reach unheard of success.

As you read, look for the example icon for real-life instances:

👀 **<u>Example:</u>**

Chapter 1

Burnarounds Have Warning Signs

Think of a *Burnaround* as the prehypertension stage of high blood pressure. You still have time to cut out the salt, go on a low-fat diet, and hit the gym. But if you don't act soon, you will move into Stage 1 turnaround.

There are seven warning signs that your company is in need of a *Burnaround*. If your company shows only one or two of these signs, you may be OK if you fix the underlying problems that gave rise to the signs. If your company shows more than two of these signs, you are in serious trouble. You need to start a *Burnaround* immediately.

Warning Sign #1—Life Is Great

You think your company is humming along just fine. You hardly ever hear of any problems. You don't even have to go to strategic meetings with your people because they take care of whatever is going on. And you finally have your managers trained. They all know you don't want to hear about problems, only solutions. After all, what do you pay these people for?

The balance sheet shows a little too much debt, but you'll work that off over time. Earnings are usually solid even though, during the last recession, things got a little shaky. You had to dip into the revolving credit line for the first time in your company's history. But, heh, that's what it's for, right? Funny thing though, the bank just raised the interest rate on you without warning. Oh, well, you'll pay that off next year.

Your customers seem happy, although a few of them have switched to your competition because of price. And you sometimes wonder why some of them don't order as much as they used to. Nevertheless, you're not worried — your salespeople tell you it will get better next quarter. Or the quarter after that. Fine, you think. Let them go with a cheaper brand.

Your employees seem content, as well they should be since you pay the highest wages around. But the factory doesn't appear to hum like it used to. Almost seems like people have slowed down — probably because they are so productive. Health care costs are way up, but so are everybody else's. Yes, sir, $140K sales-per-employee a year — right about what a Rustbelt manufacturer should be.

You feel good that you finally have the business on automatic. You can play golf while your people run the show. You don't need to make any changes because everything is going along just great.

And yet, something keeps gnawing at you.

 ## Warning Sign #2—Innovation Doesn't Live Here Anymore

Product development has been a little slow for a while. Used to be, your company continually cranked out a ton of innovations that the marketplace just loved. These days, most of your product developments are minor enhancements to existing lines that don't yield better margins. But that's OK, because the customer expects product improvements. Still, it bothers you that, while they expect improvements, they won't pay for them.

> You're thinking that it's a good thing you have your old standby products to hang on to, yet you wonder how long that can last. Probably longer than your lifetime, you think, because your products are the best.

You've heard that your industry doesn't like new things. At least that's what your sales and engineering people tell you. Their evidence is that the last several attempts at new products ended up going nowhere. Oh, they came out the other end of the pipeline all right, but hardly any of them sold…at least not very much.

Your salespeople tell you that the price is too high and the customers didn't want the products anyway. Your engineers tell you that if your salespeople were any good, they could sell the benefits. You're thinking that it's a good thing you have your old standby products to hang on to, yet you wonder how long that can last. Probably longer than your lifetime, you think, because your products are the best.

Your engineers like to design cool, new features and they like to tinker a lot. One time you asked them if a customer had ever asked them for one of these cool, new features and they looked at you like you were from Mars. It seems like they are always tinkering with a feature but little is done. Further, they complain that your marketing people should be able to sell all these cool features. Then Marketing complains that the engineers are out of touch with what the customer wants and, more important, what the customer will pay for. You haven't hired a freshly minted engineer in years. After all, why would you do that when you have these experienced engineers just sitting there?

Warning Sign #3—Your Sales Team Is on Your Customers' Payroll

Your salespeople have been around a long time. Decades, in fact. They have forgotten more about your industry than your competitors' salespeople ever knew. So it seems odd that the bad guys seem to be getting a share of your sales. But your salespeople have deep and personal relationships with your customers. They know the customers' wives, ages of their kids, even their religious preferences. They often entertain the customers, as evidenced by the hefty expense reports.

They identify with the customers more than they do with your company. When it comes to a conflict between the two, your salespeople usually side with the customer. Sometimes you wonder whose side they are on.

But that's OK, because someone needs to be the customers' advocate, right? The customer is always right, as they say. Still, it worries you a bit that your salespeople might give the customer too much. They don't seem to care whether it costs the company or not. They only want the customer to be happy. If it comes to putting a price increase through, forget it. They won't even try it. They'll sandbag you until you give up.

Your salespeople don't spend much time around the engineers or other people in the office. They believe that time spent at headquarters is wasted and that the "real" job is out there with the customers in the "real" world. Well, you think, they can't spend too much time with the customers, can they?

Yet you wonder how much time they are actually spending with the customer and if it really drives more sales.

 ## Warning Sign #4—Everyone Makes Nice in Your Meetings

Your senior-management team knows exactly how to do what they do. They don't meet with each other much, but you figure that's because they don't need to. After all, why would Manufacturing need to meet with Engineering unless there's a problem?

> Do your managers show little concern for the welfare of the group or company as a whole?

Your staff meetings are infrequent—once a month tops. You don't see the need to get folks together more often, because who wants to meet constantly? When you see an issue in a given area, you meet with that person independently. Why bother all your managers with a problem in one area?

When you *do* have staff meetings, your managers are preoccupied with their own areas. If you happen to be discussing a marketing issue, the other managers will be checking email or might even leave the room. That bothers you a little bit but, on the other hand, it shows the concern and dedication they have for their own areas. You wonder if that is to a fault.

Your managers show little concern for the welfare of the group or company as a whole. After all, they are paid to manage their own areas, not someone else's. You sometimes wish they would take a broader, more general-manager type of view.

Often, one of your managers will raise an issue with you after the group is gone. You wonder why it wasn't raised in front of the others, but you understand that sometimes these things are handled better one-on-one. There is little discussion in the staff meetings, and almost never a debate. If something starts to get a little heated, someone will suggest that it be "taken off-line" and that ends the discussion. You prefer it that way, because it doesn't take up valuable staff meeting time with side issues. Besides, you want these people to like each other, and shouting matches seem counter-productive.

 ## Warning Sign #5—Your Employees Work for Your Competition

Boy, that factory is a snake pit! Lots of salty old dogs working back there. Sometimes you feel it's best to stay out of there. Vulgar language is a way of life in your factory, as it has been for years. You see no real harm in it, because everyone expects it and can dish it out as well as they can take it. You sorta see it as a release for the tedious and repetitive tasks in manufacturing.

It seemed like harmless banter until recently when it led to fisticuffs. You ended up firing both of the people involved. It was a shame too, because they were company veterans. Well, that will teach everyone a lesson in behavior. At the end of the day, the language bothers you, but since it's been going on so long, how could you put a stop to it now?

In the office area, you've noted a lot of infighting. People within departments seem to be arguing all the time, and they hardly ever talk to people in other departments. When they do, it's usually an argument over lack of resources. Seems like people *do* meet to solve issues, but then the process breaks down when they leave the room. People treat each other disrespectfully, although perhaps not as bad as in the factory.

It seems like people can't wait to get out of the building at 5 o'clock. And you've noticed that you're about the only one in the building *after* 5:00. That seems strange, because your company certainly has many issues to work on. Oh well, if people can get their work done in eight hours, why stick around, right?

Email is the preferred method of communication, even when people have offices next to each other. (You are copied on a lot more emails than you think you should be.) Half the time, you don't even know what issue these emails are supposed to address. You wonder if you are expected to intercede in the issue, so you often do, and then wonder if your intercession helps or hurts.

 ## Warning Sign #6—Your Manufacturing Plant Is a Decade Behind

Your manufacturing manager has been producing your widgets for what seems like forever. He knows exactly how to run that factory. He does a great job in scheduling the work, purchasing raw materials, and shipping the product out.

However, it seems like a long time since he talked about cost reductions. He cites good reasons why cutting costs is hard to do, and he tells you that the answer to the problem of margins is to raise prices. Or for Engineering to redesign the products with lower cost material. His focus seems to be on cost containment, which he describes as cost increases no more than the rate of inflation. That bothers you a little, because that means your margins go down by the same amount since Sales can't get a price increase through.

Manufacturing has very little turnover. You

can't remember the last time someone was let go in the factory. You figure that's because the workforce is so experienced. Your manufacturing managers tell you they are all doing a pretty good job. Even so, you think that sales-per-employee could be improved. At $140K, it's not bad, but it is hard to imagine competing with the Chinese at that number. Thank God your customers say they refuse to buy from China, but you wonder how long that will last.

Healthcare costs are out of sight. But whose aren't? Lately you've been talking to your human-resources manager about raising deductibles and lowering the company's contribution to premiums. She doesn't want to do that because it will upset the workforce.

Worse, you have an endless stream of increasingly expensive overhead. The monthly phone bill would choke a horse. People expect raises every year. Seems like all your managers have to have an assistant. The revolving door of requests to hire more people and buy more capital equipment is unbelievable. They all claim the requests will improve productivity, but you can't find the improvements on the balance sheet. You wonder if all this overhead is really necessary.

You haven't reduced product cost in a while. In fact, with rising commodity prices, your costs have gone up. And, since your salespeople can't seem to bring a price increase to the customer, your margins have suffered.

Warning Sign #7—Your People Don't Embrace the Global Economy

You know the US market well, as do your people, because it is your *only* market, even though you are pretty sure your product could be applied internationally. The problem in the US is that margins are getting thin. You were surprised recently to learn that a foreign competitor took some business away from you. You had never heard of this company before, and your salespeople were dumbfounded. Now you're worried that they are after the rest of your business.

You have been content to let exporters handle any business outside the US. Occasionally they get a fair-sized order and export it somewhere. Sometimes you wonder what their margins are on your products, but you figure that's their business. Anything they sell is incremental to your existing business. You asked them once in what countries they sold, but they wouldn't tell you.

You have hesitated to enter international markets be cause you don't know them. You have heard that some of these markets get higher margins, but you are fairly satisfied with the margins you get now. Besides, it would take a lot to offset the expense of entering those markets. You looked around once for an international salesperson and found them hard to get and very expensive. Hardly seems like it would be worth it. Now you wonder whether other untapped markets exist for your business and why your people aren't going after them. You brought it up in a staff meeting once and were told, "We have all we can handle now." Funny though, you don't feel that way.

Chapter 2

What Is a *Burnaround*?

👀 **Example:** It was five minutes before midnight. I was dead tired from 20 hours of almost nonstop negotiating. Earlier in the day, the union announced to the people in our factory that negotiations had broken down and management had walked out. It was a lie.

My boss had been calling the hotel where we were negotiating every 30 minutes, demanding updates and wanting to know why more progress hadn't been made. The television crew and newspaper reporters were on me like a cheap suit. They were predicting the demise of the company, which had been in that city for over 100 years.

The strike deadline was five minutes away. The union was not cooperating. My own negotiating team was not cooperating. My boss was not cooperating. The lawyers were not cooperating. If the union struck, it would probably be the end of the company. If the union failed to meet our demands for concessions, it would almost certainly be the end of the company. And the end of my career. I was not having a good day.

The company was in a very weak position. It had lost most of its market share in the last decade and was bleeding red ink. Factory documentation was poor, so outsourcing the whole operation was not an option. It simply had to cut costs big time and improve operations right now, or it faced bankruptcy.

Our demands were real and were extensive. We needed to outsource roughly half the work (and subsequently lay off half the union employees), halve the number of union job classifications, freeze wages, and roll back benefits. Any one of those demands in and of itself would cause any self-respecting union to strike.

That was the easy part. Here was the tough part: When we started the negotiations, we were in the middle of being acquired by a foreign company. The foreign company (let's call them "Newco") was doing its due diligence when the union negotiations started. As if battling with a militant union wasn't bad enough, we had to contend with the eternal battle between our current owners and Newco over the outcome of the diligence. Moreover, the Newco transaction hinged on the outcome of the negotiations!

Just before the strike deadline, my boss started dictating to me how to break the dead-

lock. He was a brilliant man and a good nego-
tiator. He was also wrong. He was not close
enough to the action to dictate the deal, and I
knew that, if I let him make the rules, the company was doomed. That's when I gambled everything and moved the entire negotiating team
to an undisclosed hotel. I didn't tell my boss
until 12 hours later, when the whole thing was
over.

This was not a corpo-
rate exercise. It was not a
situation in which I could
afford to lose. Everything
was on the line. The fate of
a thousand employees
hung in the balance. Just
your average day in a
turnaround.

> **Business is a serious proposition, but most people don't see it that way.**

A company in a turnaround is in a life-and-
death situation. Turnaround companies either
have costs that are way too high or sales that
are way too low. In our case, we had both
problems—in spades.

A turnaround company is seriously
wounded and may not survive at all.

How did my union deal turnout? We got
the deal we needed and saved the company—
and my career.

I told this story to illustrate a point. Business is a serious proposition, but most people
don't see it that way, particularly most corporate types. They see business as a job, as some-

thing they do to earn their golf fees. They come in, do what they need to do to satisfy the boss (who is doing what he needs to do to satisfy his boss) and go home.

They have no heart and soul in the place. That's the reason for an earnest money deposit when you make an offer for a house. The realtor wants to be sure that you have some skin in the game. People with no investment in your game are temporary residents. No business can prosper without most, if not all, of the employees' total dedication. Each employee has to have a stake in your business. And that starts with you. *All* your skin needs to be in the game. That's why the vulture capitalists will insist on it. Not only will they want your mind and heart, but they will want your house. That will get your attention.

You have to put your full essence in your business if you want it, and you, to be successful. You can't just go through each day. You have to *create* each day. You have to eat, breathe, sleep, dream and have nightmares about your business. Worry has to keep you awake many nights.

Your business has to demand all your time. Success can't be an option—it has to be an absolute *must*. You need to treat every event in your business as the most important thing in your world. By that, I mean every single sale, small or large, has to be of major concern to you. Every lost opportunity has to be a major disaster. You have to be an absolute maniac when it comes to the results in your business. A turnaround will teach you this perspective — or it will kill you.

Example: Once, a business I ran, "Myco," lost a small bid. At only 1% of our total annual sales, this was not a life-or-death situation for the business. My employees were not happy about losing the bid, did everything they could to win it, and expressed great dissatisfaction when it was over. These employees really cared about what they were doing. But they were not prepared to go home that night and lose sleep over it...until I gave them a reason.

I told them that, if this was the beginning of a really low-cost competitor, it could be the beginning of the end for that segment of our business. Even though the bid was only 1%, if we lost 99% more, we would lose the business. (Actually, it would have taken a lot less than 99%.) In other words, I gave them a sense of urgency, even though the situation was not yet imperative. If you wait for it to become urgent, it is too late!

These employees didn't have the tiger instinct. They accepted the results of the bid and vowed to do better next time. And I believed them. But to do better next time is not good enough! As the CEO, you yourself have to treat every lost opportunity or lost piece of business as a major disaster. Because if they all add up, it *will be* a major disaster. Always remember that the leader sets the tone for the whole organization.

> Like the frog placed in slowly warming water, your employees will not realize they are boiling to death.

I instructed my employees to chase down the results until they knew who *did* win (which was not easy to do) and why they could produce this part for a lower cost than we could. Then I asked them to find a way to get our cost lower than the other company's. I told them to object to the conditions of the bid and not give up until they had to. I told my CFO to present to the group what the financial impact of losing this bid would be to the business. After I got that, I asked them how many jobs could be lost as a result of losing this bid. Losing one piece of business, even 1%, has serious long-term consequences—a spiraling effect on cost, which affects everything from the availability of R&D and capital funds to the company's ability to compete. It is huge!

But, like the frog placed in slowly warming water, your employees will not realize they are boiling to death. You must sensitize them to the impact of every single lost opportunity or sale. It is your job to get the whole organization resonating to this.

My contention is this: What if, the next time, you lose again? And if you lose the time after that? When do you realize you are in serious trouble? Probably only when it is too late. I told my people that, if someone could produce that part lower than we could, we were in serious trouble already and the time to take action and do something about it was now—not the next time.

You might say that I am obsessive or compulsive. All right, I admit it. I am both. As the old saying goes, "Just because you are paranoid doesn't mean someone isn't out to get you." Someone is out to get your business every day. To destroy your company, your employees' futures, and your very existence. So why would you want to wait until next time to do something about it?

> In a turnaround, you learn quickly that the impossible is not impossible at all.

Turnaround CEOs know something single-digit-earnings company CEOs don't: When the orbit of the business is decaying, you correct it quickly. This is a problem that all businesses have if they are not rapidly improving. The single-digit-earning company orbit is decaying slower than a turnaround, but it is decaying nonetheless. The difference is that a turnaround knows it's decaying and does something about it quickly. The stable company doesn't do anything. It either doesn't realize it is falling from the sky, or hopes for a soft landing. It wants to cling to what it has and hope nothing bad happens.

A turnaround requires doing the impossible. You have no choice. You can't afford to say something can't be done and not even try it. The criticality of the situation forces you to try almost anything to improve the situation. In a turnaround, you learn quickly that the impossible is not impossible at all. *Burnaround* companies take the same approach.

> I don't care what the pundits say about CEO's needing to think more long-term. In the long-term, everyone is dead.

One of the many things I learned while involved with turnarounds is that business is about real money. That might sound like an obvious truth, but many people in big corporations don't get it. They think business is about looking good. Or helping their boss look good. Or making their peers or subordinates look bad.

There are a million ways to make the profit-and-loss statement look good without making real cash money. The P&L doesn't mean a thing except to the extent that it generates cash.

In a turnaround, "cash is king," as an old CFO buddy of mine used to say. At my turnaround in the 90s, we were so strapped for cash that the power company would call us just before they were ready to turn off our electricity. Only then would we (could we) pay something on the bill. Now, that is real money!

Do you think that gave us a focus on expenses? Absolutely. When you are not sure if you can pay the utility bill, do you tolerate corporate overhead (i.e., unnecessary) expense? Absolutely not. You can't afford to. *Burnaround* companies understand this and watch cash and expenses as if the light bill depends on them.

When real money is at stake, it forces you to think about the business in a completely new way. If forces you to not think about not ROI, but RQROI (real quick return on investment). If forces you to think short-term. And I don't care what the pundits say about CEO's needing to think more long-term. In the long-term, everyone is dead. *Burnaround* companies treat the real money in the business as if it was their own.

If you are successful in the short-term, you will be successful in the long-term. If you concentrate on attaining real money every day, you will make real money every week. If you focus on attaining real money every week, you will make money every month. Every year. Soon you will have decades of real money.

Watch the money in your business every day by getting a report on cash and orders. Wherever you are in the world, be compulsive about this. You need to be. If you ever have a salesperson who doesn't know as much about today's orders as you do (which I did once), you need a new salesperson.

Turnarounds teach you to consider every day as the last day of your business, unless you focus on the right things. Focus on today, not a grand strategic vision five years out. Nobody knows what is going to happen in the business world five years from now. Plan each day. Write out the budget for each day's orders. Make each day's shipments. If you miss one, ensure that your organization reconciles it quickly; don't just skip it. Don't rationalize it; fix it.

Burnaround companies understand this. And, while they *do* set a strategic direction, it is affordable, realistic and doable. Do this every day and I guarantee you will be successful.

Burnaround CEOs demand 110% from every single employee or ask that employee to leave the company. They never deviate from their multistage, rigorous hiring process. If they discover they have made a hiring mistake, they cut their losses immediately. Most other companies accept what they get from their employees. A very few expect 100%.

Burnaround companies are global citizens, no matter how small they are. They understand the art of building long-term relationships with businesses in other cultures and they use that to significantly improve their sales and profits. Most other companies see relationships as a necessary byproduct of getting the deal done. They don't view the relationship *as* the deal. *Burnarounds* build cultures of their own choosing. They do not choose their culture by default. They create cultures that are values-based and serve the company's objectives. Most companies simply accept the culture they have. In fact, most companies don't even understand the culture they have. They don't think about culture as a competitive tool that, if used correctly, can differentiate them.

Burnaround companies build unique, sustainable advantages that their competition simply cannot duplicate. Period. Most companies build advantages that their competitors can easily duplicate, such as a new product, and often do.

Burnarounds have strict operational discipline. From strategic planning and annual operating plans to monthly coaching sessions, a *Burnaround* company is in control of its operations on a daily basis. While many companies do this, few measure and control on a *daily* basis. And even fewer stick to the operational procedures they do have.

A *Burnaround* company has eliminated the age-old problem of "that's not my job" and "I can't control that" by measuring and rewarding *every employee*, regardless of position or function, with one and only one number: profit. Most companies reward different functions for different outcomes. A *Burnaround* company brings the same turnaround-like intensity, urgency, focus and "every day is on the line" thinking to a healthy company. Yet a *Burnaround* is something more. It demands 110% of its employees while inspiring them to reach that goal. Sort of like the corporate version of tough love. It's about placing "Team 1" above all else, including the customer. A *Burnaround* company is opportunity-driven. At the end of the day, a *Burnaround* is all about creating an environment that ignites passion and excellence.

Chapter 3

Burnarounds Embrace Continual Change

Change is a basic element of a *Burnaround* company. If you want double-digit profits, be clear on this: Everything must change. Everything. Not just Sales or Manufacturing or Engineering. *Everything.* If you only "fix" Manufacturing, it will constantly have to battle with what you didn't change in the rest of the organization. And eventually, it will lose that battle. To get the mega-synergies of a *Burnaround,* it is crucial that every process and every person gets with the program. Get this part wrong and the rest of it won't work.

You can't build mega-profits by maintaining the status-quo. If you want to maintain your current situation, you should get a government job. The establishment is good at that. (Well, maybe not so good.) If you want huge gains in your com-

> You have to take out the ones who can't, or won't, embrace the new order.

pany, you have to make huge changes. Massive, gut-wrenching, nail-biting changes. Changes that just about everyone will hate. If most people *don't* like it, you aren't doing it right.

Start at the top. You will have to make an assessment of which of your senior managers will make the trip to the new way of doing business. I believe that most of them won't. It would be unusual for 10% to get on this track.

You have to take out the ones who can't, or won't, completely embrace the new order. The old leadership will cling for life to the old culture. They have to. If you are a new CEO, they can't afford for you to find out that they were the architects of the dumbest programs on the planet. Therefore, they have no choice but to defend their positions. Otherwise, you might conclude they are idiots and fire them.

You can't let them hang on for old time's sake. If you do, you have no chance of getting the rest of the company to change. Fire them. Do it respectfully, preserve their dignity, and give them a fair severance package, but do it.

From the minute you commit to a *Burnaround*, you need to take your message of change to the masses — frequently. Don't depend on your managers to deliver these messages; they will disappoint you. This is important for many reasons.

First, your message will resonate with some of the people — those who have been itching to see change happen at the company and are disgusted with the senseless nonsense that goes on. How do I know this? Because *every* company has senseless nonsense going on; the more successful ones just have less of it.

What is senseless nonsense? I could go on for a whole chapter about that, but I'll settle for a few examples: human-resources meetings, grievance meetings, meetings where no goals or outcomes are set and nothing is accomplished. CYA memos and emails. Politicking and positioning. Shall I go on? No, I said I wouldn't.

Cutting out the nonsense or the nonsense doers also provides you with an almost immediate boost to cash and earnings. It will send a clear message to the workforce that things really have changed; this is not just another management speech.

All successful change programs start with a great sales job. You have to prepare the minds of the changees to believe change is both necessary and possible. When you are trying to sell change, you need to cover both sides of the coin.

On the bad side, paint a vivid, but realistic, picture of the bad things that will happen if the change is not made. Do that first. Do it frequently.

This is the most important step in the process. You must encircle your team with images of the pain they will feel if the changes aren't made. If the company is in danger of being extinct, find examples of companies right in your own town that suffered the same fate. Talk about what happened to the employees when unemployment benefits ran out. Maybe your company is not in danger of being extinct, but you can easily find longer-term threats that you can use for your point. You have to remind people every day that, in the war of the business worlds, extinction can never be far away.

> You have to remind people every day that, in the war of the business worlds, extinction can never be far away.

Although the "change talk" is not a one-time event, you should kick it off with a special meeting. Post articles on the company bulletin board from the newspapers about local companies and flood your team with news about offshore competition and outsourcing of jobs. Find occasions every day for brief, but compelling, statements about why you must go through the pain of change.

People will feel the pain of change every day: the pain of lost comfort, the pain of lost power, the pain of working harder and perhaps even earning less money for it. This feeling is very real, so you need to make the symptoms of not changing real as well. You need to be sure people understand that the agony of not changing will be worse than that of changing. When people are intentionally resisting or sabotaging the change efforts, you must terminate them—loudly and publicly—to ensure that other people understand that they too might be fired for not supporting the change. That will drive the "worse pain if you don't change" message home loud and clear. Change is not optional, folks, it's mandatory.

> A time clock teaches people to do no more than time dictates, that they are machines to be used and depreciated.

Then you need to paint a vivid and attractive picture of the good things that will happen with the changes. If your company is already in trouble, the "good things" for the employees might be keeping their jobs, unlike their neighbors who did not. Get people to imagine how it will feel to be a *winner* rather than an also-ran. Profit before tax doesn't motivate most employees, but the feeling of being a winner resonates with almost everybody.

Also, provide plenty of incentives to those who go along with the program. Not only monetary, but celebratory as well. Find reasons to celebrate small wins and endeavors. Symbols are an important part of this process.

👀 **Example:** I was once sent to fix a factory that was on the verge of extinction. Productivity was very poor. Morale was even worse; many people simply didn't care. The moral contract between the factory and management was basically, "You won't pay us much or expect much from us and we won't give *you* much either." That was mainly because wages were below market and benefits were substandard.

I also had to decide the fate of the head of manufacturing. What would you do with a manager who allowed those conditions to exist? You got it; he had to go or nothing else I could do would work.

Then I took a two-pronged approach to changing this culture. First, I announced that I would no longer tolerate poor performance. And I promised them I would raise wages and benefits to market rates. We couldn't do one without the other.

I never expected to get super performance from the same people who couldn't care less yesterday until I made good on my second promise: We started firing the poor performers. In the first year, we turned over almost the entire factory, which was not such a big deal because voluntary turnover was almost 100% anyway.

As this process unfolded, I took the next step in changing the factory culture. I announced that I trusted people, so we no longer needed time clocks. I must say, however, that I've never approved of time clocks. I believe they are better-performance inhibitors. They demean people and reduce them to the stature of a machine.

How could such a practice possibly motivate people to do their best? A time clock tells people to put in *time*. They punch in and they punch out, punch in and punch out. Don't think in the middle, just punch in and punch out. A time clock teaches people to do no more than time dictates, that they are machines to be used and depreciated. Teach the machine, feed the machine, and require the machine to punch another machine. Is it any wonder that employees act like machines? You would be amazed at the gains you can make by eliminating the time clock.

I used symbolism when I announced this change. How? I gathered all the employees outside. There, in the middle of the courtyard, lying on the ground, were all the time clocks from the factory. I was holding a sledgehammer. You guessed it: I hammered every one of those time clocks. You should have heard the cheering from the employees. It was a great day, and symbolism was a big step forward in our change program.

👀 **Example:** In a division of another company, I introduced the change program using symbols from a movie. I had all the employees gathered in an auditorium for what they thought would be another boring PowerPoint speech from a suit.

At the front of the room was a boxing ring instead of a stage. By then, people were, of course, wondering what was going to happen. Suddenly the music from *Rocky* came on. I bounded onto the stage dressed in red, white and blue boxing shorts with gloves on and a red satin boxing cape! I danced around like this for several minutes before starting the meeting. When I did start the meeting, I told them we were finished as the underdog in the market. I said, just as Rocky did, that we were going to make a startling and phenomenal comeback. As you can imagine, this entrance and analogy really got their attention.

Then, throughout the year, we would give outstanding employees "knockout" awards to keep the theme and the symbolism alive. This whole theme gave people a rallying point and a cause they could believe in and be proud of. That is the secret to getting people behind your change program: Give them something bigger than themselves to believe in. Give them a cause they can feel good about, something that inspires them.

Chapter 4

Burnarounds Unleash Creative Ideas

I have tried some of the most lame-brained schemes you could imagine. At the time, of course, I thought they were all terrific. Your own ideas are always grand, aren't they? I have launched a whole bunch of super-successful new products and businesses, which were also terrific when they first appeared in my mind.

> Opinions mean nothing when it comes to a new idea—only the marketplace matters.

What was the difference between the wonderful ideas that turned out to be dogs and those that turned out to be solid gold? I have no idea—and neither does anybody else when it's only an idea.

Opinions mean nothing when it comes to a new idea; only the marketplace matters. So your job is to create the environment where you can put out blizzards of new ideas to see if they fly.

When you launch a new idea, you should feel what I call pre-performance jitters down in the pit of your gut.

👀 **Example:** I once started a trade show in a foreign country, something that had never been done, something most so-called experts said would never work. My personal financial commitment to launch it was huge, and we had no guarantee that it would be successful.

> The key is to get the ideas out there as fast as possible and let the market, not the pundits, decide.

So there I was, sitting around the convention hall the day before the exhibitors arrived, wondering if any of them would show up. Actually, I was terrified that they wouldn't. Terror is how you know the risk is worth taking.

I did all I could to mitigate this risk. Many exhibitors wouldn't place advance deposits, but I got them, and credit card guarantees, when I could. I did everything possible to limit the downside, without *limiting the upside.*

This is an important point. You can limit the downside so much that you restrict, or extinguish, the upside potential. Obviously, you don't want to do that. Bracket your appetite and ability to withstand the downside and keep the upside as unlimited as you can.

The trade show was held in January. I

could have limited the downside by requiring every exhibitor to pay in advance. Or I could have demanded that every single exhibitor put down a deposit or I wouldn't reserve the space in the exhibit hall.

Why didn't I? First, this was a new trade-show, so it didn't have the history and credibility to request such demands. Second, and most important, I would have lost a lot of customers, because many of these exhibitors are on a calendar fiscal year. That means they can't spend a dime in December and they can spend anything in January.

I have no idea how many exhibitors I would have lost, but I do know that, by trying to protect the downside, I would have severely limited the upside. If there is a limit to the upside, why would you want to do it at all?

Of course, you have to look at, and justify, the downside. But don't spend all your time there or you will wind up on the floor in the fetal position sobbing for the janitor.

How did the trade show work out? It was a spectacular success, exceeding even my highest hopes.

I can tell you just as many stories about new ideas that were absolute disasters. They key is to get the ideas out there as fast as possible and let the market, not the pundits, decide.

Your organization is bubbling with innovation and creativity. You can find it in the hallways. It is ever-present in the company cafeteria, at the water cooler, in the happy-hour watering hole. Your employees are fiercely debating these ideas.

Many people in your company are just bristling with the next generation *this* or the next generation *that*. Some of these thoughts (perhaps most of them) could propel your company into the future like you wouldn't believe. These kinds of ideas created all the innovation and achievement in our world today. Your company has this capability right now.

You're thinking, "Sure, I know what he's going to say next: All I need to do is tap into these ideas—a job easier said than done." Actually, you *can't* tap into these ideas. They were never meant for you to tap into. In fact, it's impossible for you to tap into these ideas. The ideas will tap into you when you create the conditions in your company that makes them want to.

> **Don't punish failure— celebrate it!**

Create a "fast failure" group whose job is to fail fast. Sounds weird, huh? Most companies punish people for failure. You should celebrate when it comes to *innovation*. You have to treat this effort differently from some of the other disciplines. Cost-of-sales is a quantifiable area. (No one doubts the cost of materials or people. No one ever says, "I don't believe you can't buy a commodity for x dollars." Commodity prices are known at any time and are not subject to opinion. So you can't allow your manufacturing person to fail fast all the time when he's buying commodities.)

New product ideas are a different breed of cat. Ideas are not finite science. How the market will react to a new idea is not quantifiable. The only way to deal with the idea is by shooting it out there and seeing what happens. You will never be able to do that if you don't create the conditions in your company that facilitate and reward it.

Don't allow people to express opinions about a new product idea unless they can back the idea up with hard facts, but don't let anyone kill an idea until it has time to bloom. As the CEO, you have to set the tone here.

You need to reframe, in your own mind, what you believe is possible, then help your organization do the same.

> **Create the conditions to win the battle for control of what your organization accepts as possible.**

👀 **Example:** Some people think it is impossible to walk on a bed of hot coals (2,000 degrees Fahrenheit, plus or minus a few degrees here and there) without horribly disfiguring their feet. Do you think you could do that? I used to think it was impossible. Until one day, I thought it *was* possible, so I did it at an Anthony Robbins motivational workshop. I liked it so much that I did it four times over several years. I guess I had to keep convincing myself it was possible. Then I took my whole team to Chicago and we did the fire walk together. You can't imagine the juice they got from that experience. And tons of creative ideas came as a direct result of it.

Why on earth would I want to do such a fool thing? It's simple: I wanted to win the battle for control of what my mind and my employees' minds can believe is possible. Therein lies the heart of the matter. Your mind is conditioned to believe that anything that hasn't been done is impossible. Your organization may be conditioned this way as well.

Create the conditions to win the battle for control of what your organization accepts as possible. Bring in what I call "mind benders" to challenge your and your organization's assumptions and beliefs. This is not a one-time event. "Mind bend" your company often.

Chapter 5

Burnarounds Build Global Relationships

I once accomplished a deal that, on the surface, seemed to be a very simple agreement. In the United States, I could have done this deal in three meetings over about two months. The outcome took a year, over a dozen face-to-face meetings, and endless teleconferences. I can't tell you how many times I threw my hands up and concluded that we would never get a deal. We had cultural, language and legal obstacles. Which obstacle do you think was the most important and difficult to overcome? You got it— the cultural obstacles.

The reason it took so long was that I spent a lot of time building a relationship with the principals in the foreign company long before we ever got the lawyers involved. After the deal was

> If the other side thinks you screwed them on the deal, they won't help you.

done, I spent another ton of time maintaining and improving that relationship.

After the agreement was concluded, we almost immediately began modifying it to suit conditions we did not anticipate during the negotiations—something that often happens post-deal. That's why you have to build the relationship and work the deal from a fair-to-both-sides perspective.

I was criticized up and down throughout this process. People wanted to know why it was taking so long. People thought I gave too much. My people said I went to their country too often instead of the other team's coming to us. (They did come to the United States once in a while.) People told me I should have given up because the foreign team wanted too much. Many people told me I should have walked away because the negotiations were too hard. And indeed they were. However, because I understood their fears, I knew their intentions were good.

> **Mr. Lincoln found it quite odd that God gave her all the answers, but gave him the job.**

That story reminds me of something Abraham Lincoln said during the Civil War. He was responding to a letter from a constituent who frequently wrote him to criticize his actions. She thought she knew better how to run the war (from her parlor). Mr. Lincoln wrote her back that he thought it was quite odd that God gave her all the answers, but gave him the job. Always remember that. It is easy to criticize when you are not responsible for the outcome. It doesn't mean you are right, but it does mean you have the job. Please don't forget that advice when you are tempted to criticize someone else's attempts.

We inked the deal in their country, even though United States law governed the agreement. And, while the signing could have been done by fax, I traveled 6,000 miles to sign the agreement personally. Why? Two very important reasons: One, I did not want them to find a minor reason not to sign. I figured that outcome was less likely if I were there. Second, I wanted to keep stressing my commitment to the venture. And, as a symbolic but important gesture, I even signed the papers using their company pen, which I brought with me just for that occasion. They didn't miss this symbolism; they said it was just one more example of the strength of the new-found partnership.

This deal is a perfect illustration of your garden-variety international deal. *Burnaround* companies understand that emails and faxes don't come to agreement—people do.

> *Burnaround* companies are constantly expanding their network of global relationships and partnerships.

The *Burnaround* company is constantly expanding its network of global relationships and partnerships. In the international market, relationships are everything. You must build the affinity first, and the business comes later.

Some people call this process "relational capital." Like all capital assets, there are costs associated with acquiring them. However, unlike capital assets that depreciate whether you maintain them or not, relational capital grows in value if maintained and nurtured.

Diversifying your business into international markets is a hedge against US economic cycles because profits are generally better in many international markets than in the United States. Especially if you are a small business, because your competition is unlikely to go abroad.

Your competition might not go after the global market because they think it's hard. It is. Your competition probably thinks building global relational capital is expensive. It is. Chances are that your competition has delegated what little international business they have to an agent or an export management company. That's OK to do in the beginning, while you get your feet wet. However, if your product has any application in international markets, you'll want to sell it directly, at the right time, and cut out the middleman. You can't do this until you've built your global relational capital.

Many US companies just don't bother with such relationship building. They can't understand why other countries don't subscribe to what I call "cowboy deal making": Ride into town, negotiate hard and get everything you can (at least more than the other side does), shoot 'em up, and ride out. This approach is intensely disliked by the international market and hugely ineffective.

> Most US companies use "cowboy" deal-making.

Task your organization with finding and building global relational capital. Quantify the purpose by including a certain number to be *initiated* (not *completed* — remember, you don't want to do "cowboy deals") in a given year. I think two is a good number for most small companies. It is a doable number without appearing too pushy to the potential international partners.

Expect results to be slow. Building global relational capital and the business that follows is a multiyear effort. Expect no return for the first three years. You read that right: no results. I promise you that the results will follow in incremental sales and profit. Even in a small business, you can achieve 20% of your total sales from international business. In addition, the margins on these sales should be at least 25% higher than your United States margins.

Remember, a *Burnaround* company builds

unique sustainable advantages that the competition can't duplicate. Period. Building global relationships is one of them.

Chapter 6

Burnarounds Have a Secret Weapon

Professional football teams all have individual players who are outstanding athletes. They are tough, smart, conditioned, lean, mean fighting machines. Pound for pound, player for player, there probably isn't much difference between individual players from one team and the other. But the better "team" will win most of the games. Not because of individual superstars — because the *team* is the champion.

A world-class orchestra is a team of gifted musicians, and the job of each musician is to produce a world-class performance. You don't see the violin section saying, "We don't care what the brass section did, we did our job." No single musician or section is a superstar. The orchestra *team* is the champ.

> The *team* is the champion.

A world-class surgical team may contain a particularly gifted surgeon, but most surgeons will tell you that the *team* is the superstar. You don't hear the anesthesiologist saying, "Hey, my only job is to put this guy to sleep; the rest of it is not my problem."

> We all play on a level field when it comes to the capital side of business.

So why do so many businesses allow each individual function to be isolated from the whole? Why do so many senior managers think their job is done when they have engineered the widget, constructed the widget, or sold the widget?

Your competition is driving cost improvements and value engineering every day of the week. So what else is new? You have been doing that for years. Your competition has earmarked 6% of sales for R&D; nothing new for you here either. We all play on a level field when it comes to the capital side of business.

So, with all those equalizing factors, how on earth do you win?

Burnaround companies know some things single-digit-earning companies don't. *Burnarounds* understand that the only sustainable, not easily duplicated, competitive advantage is well-operating teams — from the top to the bottom of the organization. They understand that the "people quotient" is the most important asset in the business.

The people quotient is not a platitude or a slogan in a *Burnaround* company. They invest inordinate money, time and attention in getting this part right. Their factories are self-directed. Their employees live by purposeful values that serve the company. Those values are more than banners on the walls. Politics do not exist in *Burnaround* companies. Employees are treated like valued members of a team, almost like family. *Burnaround* companies inspire their employees to reach ever-higher performance—and they get it.

Your competition has lots of smart people, and so do you. Your competition is well capitalized, and so are you. Your competition has many patents, and so do you. Your competition pays competitively and hires good talent, and so do you.

An excellent senior-management team is the one factor that can give any company greatness. At the end of the day, the only sustainable competitive advantage you have could be your

> The most important job of a CEO is to build a world-class team.

team. Are they individual players trying to score, or are they putting the ball in the hands of the person in the *best position* to score? When they come out of the huddle, do they run the play the quarterback called or do they go off and do their own thing? Is your team comprised of a bunch of stars or is the team the star? These are important questions you should be addressing.

In my view, the most important job of a CEO is to build a world-class team. This sounds easy when you read about it, but let me tell you, it's tough. Especially if you are trying to forge a team of newly collected people or get an existing "staff" to work as a "team."

Few companies use this lever because it is harder than hell for it to work. It takes a huge dose of reality when confronting the brutal facts. It takes guts to do something about the facts once you learn them. It's a contact sport to get up close and personal when demanding, and expecting, that your senior managers play on the senior-manager team, not their own. Hard, yes, but good news for you if you accomplish it.

👀 **Example:** Years ago, I led a group of senior managers that I thought were not performing well as a team. Yet, in their minds, they were all doing their jobs. The head of sales was calling on customers. The manufacturing manager was putting out widgets. The finance manager was counting the widgets. Engineering was, well, engineering. So what's not to like about that, you say?

My first clue about the lack of teamwork came while sitting through senior-management meetings and observing rather than participating. Conflict was noticeably absent. No debates ever occurred, passionate or otherwise. The meetings were quiet and polite. Sometimes I wasn't sure if I was looking at a room of senior managers or an oil painting! Occasionally an issue would be raised, not solved, and then dismissed. "Let's take it off-line," they would say. No one took accountability for mistakes. As far as they were concerned, there were no mistakes. (See Warning Sign #4.)

👀 **Example:** Once my team launched a product that was a total failure, and I asked for a post-mortem. When we did that, my sales guy concluded the analysis with a proclamation that he couldn't find anything we did wrong. All the other managers agreed. The product met the functionality targets. It met the cost and price targets. Yet it was a total failure.

> A dysfunctional senior-management team is a dirty little secret no one wants to own up to.

How could anyone conclude that we did nothing wrong? How about never starting the darn thing to begin with?

I voiced my concerns, and said that I wanted to get outside help for teambuilding and communications improvement, and I asked them for their feedback on the need for it. Every one of them denied the existence of a problem. Each told me that, while there might be some minor issues, they certainly didn't need to get outside help to fix them. They asked me for specific examples.

I had no shortage of examples. I went with them point-by-point on what I had observed. I named names and called them like I saw them. Project failings, communication failures, missed commitments, the whole ball of wax. My team had a huge wart and they couldn't even see it. Or wouldn't admit it.

If your face has a blemish, chances are that you can't see it either. But everybody else can. No one will tell you about this wart because they want to be polite. They have to work with you, side by side, every day, so they don't want to risk upsetting you. That would cause tension in the workplace. Heaven knows, we can't have that. Let's have a nice, happy place.

Since no one will tell you, you keep chugging along—dumb and happy, warts and all, thinking nothing is wrong. No one on my senior-management team wanted to tell the others about this wart. Everyone wanted things to be just peachy.

The fact that the senior-management team was dysfunctional was a dirty little secret no one wanted to own up to. And many managers didn't think it was their problem as long as they and their functions were doing their jobs.

Remember, everyone at Pearl Harbor was doing their job when the Japanese attacked; everyone in our government was doing their job on 9/11. If your team of managers is just doing their job, your business is in big trouble.

Here's why nobody wants to come out of the closet. If your senior managers admit to the boss that there is a problem, then they have to also take accountability for the problem. How did they let it get that way? What are they going to do about fixing

> As the emperor, you have to assume at all times that you have no clothes.

it? They are afraid they will be blamed. After all, does anybody want to admit to the boss that there is a problem?

Well, I, for one, wish they would admit it more often. I can't tell you how many times I have walked into an ambush that could have been avoided if someone had told me. As the emperor, you have to assume at all times that you have no clothes, because usually no one will tell you.

This is a critically important point. If you have the top job, you can make a million stupid decisions and most people will smile and tell you how smart you are. When these stupid decisions fail miserably, you have only yourself to blame.

Even though my senior managers denied any problems, I asked each of them to anonymously rate the team in the areas of teamwork, focus, communication and accountability. Not surprisingly, most scores were C's, a few D's, one B. Remember, this was from the team that said there were no problems! Or perhaps the deeper problem was the team believed a C was an OK score. Or, even worse, they knew about the problem but didn't think it was important enough to fix. Now I don't know about you, but if I have to have major surgery, I would rather not have the D team do it.

One of your key roles as CEO is to help your team face the ugly truth. The ugly truth in my case was that the senior-management team was a C minus.

> Dealing with a dysfunctional team might be the hardest thing you have to do.

Dealing with a dysfunctional team might be the hardest thing you have to do. Don't be gentle or subtle about this; gentle and subtle won't work. You need to hit your players with a baseball bat. Then you will have to hit them harder with a brick. This lack of facing the ugly truth is why Wang is not around anymore. It's what happened to IBM and countless other companies, large and small. Don't let it happen to you. And don't ever forget: Both the beautiful and the ugly truth change. What looks good today might become tomorrow's monster.

My senior managers viewed teambuilding as holding hands and singing *Kumbaya*. At best, they saw it as an extracurricular activity to satisfy the boss. The sooner they could be done with it and get on with the real work, the better. My most senior manager showed open disdain for the teambuilding process we went through.

I asked each of my senior managers, "What is your job?" My sales guy said his job was to get orders. The head of engineering said his job was to produce new designs. Manufacturing said to construct widgets. Wrong, wrong, and wrong.

This is where I differ from traditional models of senior-management teams. The job of your senior managers is to be a senior-management team. Your senior salesperson's primary role is being a member of the senior-management team. His first allegiance needs to be with *that* team, not the sales team. Of course, it is his job to *lead* the sales function; he is the coach. But he does not play on the sales team. His primary focus should be participating with the rest of the senior-management team in leading the *company*, not the sales function.

> If your team gets out of control, the fault is always yours, not theirs.

I call it "Team 1." Team 1's primary function is to increase profit and shareholder value. What is the second most important task of Team 1? To increase profit and shareholder value. That is the job of *every* employee in your company.

Salespeople, in particular, have a problem with this. They think their first allegiance should be to the customer. After all, they say, "The customer pays the bills." Whenever I hear that, I quickly correct them. Customers do *not* pay the bills — *profit* pays the bills.

I took my senior managers through an intensive teambuilding process, with the aim of moving to the Team 1 model. I don't mean roasting marshmallows and rock climbing together. I mean a painful examination of how we behaved rather than how we *should* behave as a senior-management team. Don't do this by yourself; get a professional facilitator who is good at this sort of thing.

As we worked through the half-day, twice-a-month sessions, it became clear that the team was gravely dysfunctional. Whose fault was that? Mine. Remember, if your team gets out of control, the fault is always yours, not theirs.

What was my outcome? After several months of counseling, I fired one executive from the team and reassigned another.

Note that I said several *months*, not *years*. Executive management is a contact sport. Don't coddle these people. Tell it to them straight, give them a short leash to fix it, then boot them out if they can't, or don't want to, fix it. That is your job.

Many CEOs don't have the stomach for this. You need fortitude, because this process gets personal for your most senior people. Be ready to fire anybody on your senior team that doesn't go along with the program.

Of course, you give the team members a chance and some time to change (not much time; remember that the market isn't waiting around for you). You provide extensive counseling, in which a spade is called a spade. But you get on with it as fast as possible, because your company's life depends on the outcome.

You will get quantum benefits from implementing the Team 1 model. The entire company will observe it and model your senior management's team behavior. Processes, costs, communications — everything will improve dramatically.

And don't think that, just because you've created this killer team, your job is over. Creating the team is only the beginning. You have to continue to nurture, strengthen, reinforce, challenge and sometimes cajole it.

All teams get a little loose and a little sloppy if they aren't tweaked from time to time. And most teams won't even recognize they are getting sloppy — or they may not want to admit it. It's your job as the leader to recognize sloppiness when it happens (and trust me, it will happen) and do something about it. Fast.

How will you know it when you see sloppiness? Here's a checklist and a "mini" prescription for each.

• Answers to important questions are not crisp. Demand crisp, clear, quantifiable, accountable answers to every question asked.

• You hear, fuzzy, noncommitted answers

like "I'm not sure when that will get done." Don't ever accept that as an answer so you can set the expectation that everyone should be prepared with measureables in the future.

• You hear, "I haven't heard" when asking the status of a new customer initiative. That means the person is relying on the other party in the transaction to do the follow-up. Each team member must be accountable for their own follow-up. You hear this a lot from sales-people. They don't want to bother their customers, so they wait for the customer to do the follow-up. Don't let them get away with that. If the initiative is important to the customer, they shouldn't mind follow-up. If it's not, you shouldn't be doing whatever it was you were following up on to begin with.

• You start to hear "my guess is" or "I think" too much. Guesses have no place in the answer to a business question or as part of a business analysis. And no one cares what you, I or anybody else *thinks*. Insist that your team have solid quantifiable facts and answers to business questions. Whenever I hear those responses, I stop the discussion until we get facts, not guesses, in our hands.

• Team meetings just seem to go a little too smoothly. This is a hard area to put your finger on, but when the meetings seem like there just isn't enough controversy or debate, it's a sign that the team is getting sloppy. Over time, even the best teams will start to fall back into the comfort zone of "nice-nice." The purpose of a team is not to be nice to each other. The purpose of a team is to be effective. That often involves challenging each other, calling each other out, raising objections and questioning what another team member may be doing.

👀 **Example:** My senior management team and I were reviewing the annual operating plans (AOP) each had submitted for approval. My product development guy had 9-10 new product developments (that were given to him by the sales guys) on his AOP. Want to know how many of those new product developments were on the sales teams AOP? Zero, nada, zip, none. Now bear in mind that we are all sitting in the same room during this review and the product development guy didn't take the sales team to task for not having these new developments in their operating plans. I stopped the meeting right then and there and took sales to task for not having the products on their AOP. Remember: There can be no accountability without visibility. Without those developments on the sales AOP, the development team will expend lots of expense and activity without any accountability or commitment to get sold.

If you see those behaviors creeping into your team, spike them quickly. What I usually do is get the teams offsite for a day or two. Then I make them face the ugly truth. Be prepared for them not to like this conversation because, up until now, they imagined themselves as the all-star team from heaven. And now you're telling them they are the no-star team from hell (well, maybe not that bad, but you get the point).

I lay out the problem by describing the view from 30,000 feet, and the specific behaviors (with examples) I see that are the root cause. I spend a lot of time trying to get them to see what I see. That is important because, if you don't, the teams will give window dressing to the meeting and keep doing things the same way. Then we agree on specific behavioral changes and set a date for getting offsite again to do see if the changes we agreed to are working. I usually like to do that in three to four months. In the meantime, if any of the old behavior rears its ugly head, I spike it right away to remind everyone of the commitments they made to the new behavior.

Chapter 7

Burnarounds Demand 110% from Every Single Employee

It's amazing how many people in the world do everything they can to do as little as they can to just barely get through the day. Are you one of those? Or are you one of those winners who *create* their days? I think you're one of the latter or you wouldn't have bought this book.

Look at your employees. How motivated are they to do their best? Do they drag themselves in with a scowl on their face, and drag themselves out at the stroke of 5:00? I suggest to you that 98% of the business world consists of day-draggers: Get by. Keep the boss happy. Get to the bowling alley on time.

The power of one single employee to make or break your business is unbelievable.

👀 **Example:** My family and I spent a night in a brand new, beautiful hotel. The rooms were well appointed in marble and stone. An exquisite pool/spa area. A spacious lobby with double-sided fireplaces and terrific home-baked chocolate-chip cookies. This hotel had to cost something north of $10 million to construct. Heaven knows how many thousands of dollars they spent on advertising and conducting the grand opening. All this, and just one employee nearly convinced me never to return.

I was in the elevator when a woman who delivered room-service meals stepped in. She had a terrible attitude, and actually complained to me that management sometimes required her to cook the food in addition to delivering it. She hated it, she hated them and, by the sounds of it, she hated me too.

She spent the entire elevator ride telling me how rotten her job was, whether I wanted to know or not. Boy, I couldn't wait to get room service after that (not)! Just one employee and her attitude could have wrecked my whole customer experience. And not only for me. How many other people did she complain to that night?

Imagine that: They spend $10 million on a hotel and leave its fate in the hands of a disgruntled, poorly paid, obviously poorly supervised employee. Does that make any sense? That woman should be fired. The hotel manager should be fired for not canning her already.

You might say that the supervisor could not possibly know about her attitude that night. I say poppycock. Every supervisor knows which employees have bad attitudes. The problem is that they don't do anything about it.

Here's another example from the same hotel. Only this is an example of how the power of one employee convinced me to give the hotel another chance even after the poor experience with the room-service woman.

About 10 PM, we discovered that our sleeper couch had no sheets or pillows. We figured for sure that, even if we called the front desk, we would be lucky to get anything at all that late. By now, we had pretty much decided we would never come to that hotel again.

Do you think that, if hotel employees were expected to give 110% (and hired, trained, and supervised that way), those conditions could possibly exist? Does an employee giving 110% forget the sheets for the sleeper couch? No way. Only an employee just trying to get by could forget those sheets.

I couldn't help but notice something else. The lobby-area housekeeper kept a checklist telling employees exactly what to clean and how to clean it. The brass was to be polished, the floor was to be mopped, the fixtures were to be dusted. Each checklist contained a little box for the employee to check off when done.

> The problem with a checklist is that it usually encourages a 70% effort.

The problem with a checklist like that is that it

usually encourages a 70% effort. It encourages employees to do only what is on the checklist. No, sir, if it's not on the checklist, I don't have to do it. In fact, if it's not on the checklist, I am not *supposed* to do it. Maybe I'm not even *allowed* to do it.

But back to my story about the sleeper couch with no sheets. Unbelievable as it was, within five minutes, someone was there with the sheets and the pillows—and a cheery disposition with a great big smile. He apologized profusely for the inconvenience, even though he was not the idiot that forgot the sheets to begin with.

He took full accountability for someone else's blunder. And with a smile! Now that's 110%! That one employee salvaged our business for this hotel chain. Despite our previous bad experience with "Miss I don't like to cook," we will give that hotel another try. That is the power of one single employee!

Imagine how terrific your business would be if all your employees were like that. So the question you have to ask yourself is: Why aren't you working on a plan right now to turn every one of your employees into 110%-ers?

I know what you're thinking. "It's unreasonable to expect all my people to give 110%. People work a fair day for a fair wage, right?" Maybe that's the way it used to be but, in the war of the business worlds, a fair day just doesn't cut it anymore.

👀 **Example:** My first real job was at a sand-and-cement company. I worked on a sandbagging line with two older men who had been doing this job for decades. These were the kind of guys with dreams of a Budweiser at the end of the shift. You know the type I mean: They knew exactly how to put in the least work for the money.

I, on the other hand, had this crazy notion that you should work as hard and fast as you can for the money. Something I learned from my parents. So there I am, pumping iron and filling bags of sand to beat the band. However, the others straightened me out in a hurry. They explained to me that I wasn't going to get any extra money for working harder. When that didn't change my behavior, they explained to me that, if I didn't slow down, they would look bad and the boss would expect *them* to work harder. When that didn't work, they threatened to beat the daylights out of me. That worked.

> You must eliminate better-performance inhibitors.

Organizational dynamics are a lot like the white corpuscles in your body. They attack a threatening organism. A new kid on the block who wants to raise the bar and work for the highest common denominator will be attacked by the white corpuscles of mediocrity. Then everyone can get back to being below average and comfortable.

This is a perfect example of what happens every day in corporate America. Because your supervisors and managers allow mediocrity to exist anywhere, it exists *everywhere*. Water seeks its own level. You simply can't allow mediocrity to exist—period. You must stamp it out wherever you find it.

You must also eliminate what I call "better-performance inhibitors"—anything that stands in the way of performance improvement. And I mean anything—from employee morale to poor attitude to lack of adequate ventilation. You will find inhibitors everywhere you look—all you have to do is *look*.

👀 **Example:** Alex Beezlebum is a better-performance inhibitor. He hates the company. He hates his job. He hates his coworkers. He hates his wife. He hates you. There is no way on God's green earth that Alex Beezlebum is ever going to come close to improving his performance. It doesn't matter what tools or training you give him.

You can incentivize him all day long and it won't make any difference. You can gain-share with him, give him employee stock ownership, communicate competitive threats, have a company picnic and a beer bash. It won't matter what you do, Alex Beezlebum is a professional better-performance inhibitor. There is only one thing to do with Alex Beezlebum: fire him.

Period.

Is it possible that you can change Alex Beezlebum's attitude? No, no and no. Even if you were able to do so, it would take longer than you have on this earth to do it. You can't change better-performance inhibitors — you must eliminate them.

> You must have a zero tolerance policy for foul, vulgar, abusive or disrespectful language.

Another inhibitor is the quality and quantity of communications in your company. Some people think that good communications make for better performance. I don't know if that's true or not. I believe good communications are needed but are not enough. Poor communications are definitely a better-performance inhibitor, however.

I am not necessarily talking about employee meetings and group meetings. I'm talking about the day-to-day interaction between managers and employees and between employees and employees. The quality of communications in a company determines how successful the company is. Human interaction is affected mainly by doing or speaking. How your employees speak to each other determines a great many things, from morale to productivity. If the language people use with each other is respectful and constructive, morale and performance tends to be high.

On the other hand, if the way your employees (or you, for that matter) talk to each other is disrespectful, rude and not constructive, it will lower performance.

You must have a zero tolerance policy for foul, vulgar, abusive or disrespectful language in your company. I've done this, and you would be amazed at the difference in performance and morale. Notice I did not install a fancy performance-improvement program; I simply eliminated a better-performance inhibitor.

Another productivity inhibitor is a manager with his/her head up the you-know-what. I can't think of anything that will ruin better performance faster than a poor manager. What makes a poor manager? She worries more about the boss than the employees, sits in her office hoping nobody comes to her with problems, and thinks communication is a four-letter word. Ms. Smarty-Pants Know-It-All.

Who wants to work their heart and soul out for a hack like that? Nobody. You can hold all the better-performance improvement programs you want but, as long as Ms. Smarty Pants is in charge, it will go nowhere. You have to let her go. You should have fired her long ago for other reasons.

What about policies at all? I guarantee you, without even knowing you, that

> Policies rob people of their drive and inhibit performance.

your company has too many polices. Policies rob people of their drive. They inhibit performance, so why do you have so many? Because you hired people to write them. After all, human-resource people have to do *something*, so let's write lots of policies! I'm not saying that you shouldn't have policies. All I'm saying is: Keep them to a minimum.

Let's assume that you buy into the "everybody needs to be a star" approach. How do you get change going? It's a lot easier when you first take over a company but, even if you've been the CEO awhile, you can still do it. You can explain to the troops that the competition and the marketplace just got a whole lot meaner.

That will be the truth no matter when you tell it. Be very deliberate about this. This will be one of the most important presentations of your business life, so get it right. You have to "sell" your team on the concept. First, you have to scare them about what will happen to them if they don't get on board (but make it real, not fantasy). Then you have to sell them on the notion that, as a team, they are up to the challenge, and give them plenty of hope and optimism.

Explain the consequences of not getting a lot better faster. Be realistic and honest about this. This won't be hard to do when you consider the jobs America loses everyday to other countries. Don't let the corporate health and happiness weenies get in your way on this one. They will try, of course, because they don't want you to upset the employees. If you don't upset them with the facts, you aren't doing your job right. Now is not the time for sugar-coating. Their careers and economic futures depend on their buy-in.

Then tell people that, from this day forward, nothing less than a 110% effort will be acceptable. 110% is the new standard by which people will be measured. Do this carefully and one on one but, when the inevitable question arises, "What happens if I don't?" the answer has to be, "You won't be here anymore."

The next question will be, "How much more will I be paid?" The answer to that is, "You get to keep your job. Consider yourself lucky because you've been working at 70% for 100% pay."

Make no mistake. This plan will be tough sledding. People will test you right away, and the rest of your team will be watching. You will have to fire people who can't, or won't, meet the new standard (which is reasonable and attainable). Also, be mindful that there are people in the organization who have been giving 110% (they have to, since the rest are giving 70%) and are bitterly resentful that you haven't done anything about the others.

You might have to turn over most of the organization and bring in new people who are up to the task. That's OK; it's called "manage-

ment by managing." What you have been doing up to now is "management by being
there." A trained monkey can do that.

Chapter 8

Burnarounds Eliminate the Enemies Within

One of my least favorite things is corporate politics. No single factor is more life threatening to a company. As CEO, your job is to find and stamp out corporate politics wherever you find it. You will find it everywhere you look — if you *look*.

On the other hand, politics is one of my favorite things to write about. I am passionate about this subject because it is the biggest threat to corporate prosperity, and even survival in some cases like a turnaround. And perhaps the most severe aspect of corporate politics is the enemies within.

> Politics is the biggest threat to corporate prosperity.

The business world is a dangerous place. The marketplace is full of people who are intent on destroying your company. The competition does this for a living. In some cases, your customers will drive you to the brink of extinction if you let them. Add to that the govern-

77

ment, and it is a wonder any company can survive. All this pales in comparison with the power of the enemies within your company.

The larger the company, the more dangerous the enemies are. The opposition within is working to destroy you. Curiously enough, the more trouble your company is in, and the more change that's needed, the more ferociously the enemies rise to defeat you.

> **The enemies within are working every day to destroy your company.**

The antagonist is an underground organization that works by stealth. It can't survive in the light of day. It's like an international terrorist organization, working in the shadows where it can't be identified and dealt with. It attacks where you least expect it. Don't anticipate the enemies within to publicly declare war on your company. If they did, they would be easy to find and eliminate.

This adversary works by deceit and deception. It reminds me of the old 60's song, "They smile in your face, all the while they want to take your place...the back stabbers." The enemies within smile in your face. "Yes boss, this is something we need to do," having no intention of doing what you want. But, oh, how they play the game.

👀 **Example:** I remember an executive I worked with once. The CEO would mandate something to the organization. A short time later, this executive (who was perceived as very powerful and believed to be at the right hand of the throne) would subtly go through the organization and undo what the CEO was trying to do.

He would tell people that what they thought the CEO wanted was not what he wanted at all. He would "interpret" what the CEO really meant. Just that subtle action would dilute the CEO's efforts at best, and scuttle it completely at worst.

The enemies within are adept at putting roadblocks in the way. They will say, "Yes, this is a good idea, but we need to study it further. Let's form a cross-functional task force and get some focus groups going. How about a customer survey?" Yes, let's get all kinds of activity going around this initiative to be sure it dies before it ever sees the light of day.

Who are the enemies within? They are the people who feel threatened by ultra-competents in the organization. In most organizations, you will find a bell-shaped curve.

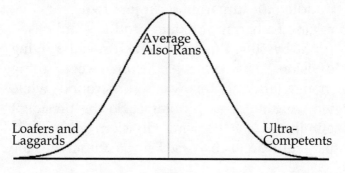

On the left side of the curve are the loafers and laggards. (The first thing you have to ask yourself is why you have anyone on your team that fits this profile.)

Under the curve are the minions of also-rans. These are the nine-to-fivers who put in a reasonable amount of work, but can't be expected to fall on a sword for the business or stick their necks out because the enemies within will declare war on them if they do. In most cases, this group is pretty safe from the death squad because they have no intention of excelling at anything.

On the right side of the curve are the ultra-competents—the movers and shakers who propel the business forward. These are the heroes of your company. They see possibility where others see impossibility. They run *through* walls, not *around* them. They are the lifeblood of your company. That's why the death squad feels compelled to eject them.

👀 **Example:** I once formed and led an elite team of ultra-competents in, of all places, the middle of a turnaround. In just two years, we released a barrage of killer products and raised profit by 50%. We pretty much saved a dying division. The other divisions were losing money (after all, this was a turnaround) while we were twice as profitable. So the president eliminated the growing division, gave me a parachute, and dispersed my team among the also-ran divisions.

How could the star division of the company be cut in favor of the dogs? Simply put, when a new CEO took over the company, the enemies within convinced him to eliminate us.

The death squad had been working on assassinating my division almost from the beginning of its formation. The more successful we were, the more rabid their efforts became. While the old CEO was there (the man who gave me the mandate to resuscitate that part of the business), he gave us cloud cover. He understood the true intentions of the enemies within and allowed us the freedom to do what was needed. And the results showed it.

I must admit, we tended to be a bit arrogant at times. Maybe a lot arrogant. That was my mistake. I should have played the corporate-politics game a little better. Unfortunately, because this was a turnaround, I didn't think we had time for that. The problem was that the rest of the organization did not believe we were *in* a turnaround. In the face of all the facts, the rest of the company thought everything was just peachy-keen. And they acted that way.

I also believed it was necessary to instill an elitist mentality in my team to give them the passion and energy they would need to mount the fierce battle ahead. I did not underestimate the enormous challenge we faced. Our customer literally hated us. Our deliveries were deplorable. Customer service was nonexistent. Product quality was poor.

When I first went into the field to meet my new customers, some of them refused to even grant me a meeting! One of them asked me what turned out to be a very poignant question: "Did your company put you into this position so they could find a reason to fire you?"

This was all against the backdrop of a company that was getting closer to death by the minute. As you can imagine, we had to move fast. No time to play politics — or so I thought.

One of the things I learned from that experience was that the enemies within are infinitely more dangerous than the enemies without.

We found that rapidly introducing new killer products was easy. We learned that beating the competition was a piece of cake. But beating the enemies within proved to be an impossible task.

I'll almost guarantee that you have this situation in your company. You don't have to be in a turnaround to have this death squad roaming the halls. You have enemies within who are trying to wipe out your ultra-competents and strangle your company. Stopping them is job

> Keep your superstars' efforts and achievements secret from the rest of the organization as much as possible.

one. It is your job as the leader to stamp out the enemies within, nurture your ultra-competents and create more superstars.

Give your ultra-competents a cloud cover. Move them off-site if you have to. Form a separate corporation if that is what it takes. And if you do, for God's sake, don't let anyone touch them—for anything. Don't let the corporate functions have anything to do with them. That means that they don't get progress reports or audits (aside for financial audits, of course). That means that the corporate staff does not get the right to review their work. Don't even let the other staff in their building!

I also recommend that you keep your superstars' efforts and achievements secret from the rest of the organization as much as possible. Unless the rest of your company feels secure in their own competence, any news of successes will represent a threat.

> Strategy needs to be realistic, affordable, and doable.

This is why so many companies set up skunk works, intended to keep the corporate meddlers out of the way and protect the ultra-competents from the enemies. While that is all well and good, it is still treating the symptom, not the cause. The cause is the enemies within. Eradicate them and you will have a much healthier company.

Chapter 9

Burnarounds Have Strict Operational Discipline

Smaller companies tend not to be as disciplined as they should be. *Burnaround* companies know that a business that is not frequently measured and course-corrected is not a business in control.

Start with an affordable, realistic, doable strategic plan—precisely what most strategic plans are not.

Teaching you how to build a strategic plan is beyond the scope of this book. Suffice it to say, you need to start with a plan to be sure your business is going forward on a purposeful path. When your team develops the plan, insist that it meets the criteria of affordable, realistic and doable.

> Review the major planks of your strategic plan, and the detailed plans of how the annual operating plan is supporting it, once a month.

As the CEO, these are the "touch points" of

operational discipline that you should be directly involved in:

(1) Once a year participate in developing and reviewing the strategic plan, annual operating plan, and budget needed to support both.

(2) Develop the annual operating plan to support the major planks of the strategic plan. The operating plan is, by nature, more detailed. A *Burnaround* company will review the major planks of its strategic plan, and the detailed plans of how the annual operating plan is supporting it, once a month. Are you reaching the goals that support your strategic plan? If not, act to get back on track.

(3) Once a week, hold a 30-minute meeting with the senior-management team to share any major pieces of information or issues the entire team should be aware of. By the way, my philosophy is that the entire senior-management team needs to be aware of most information or issues. That doesn't mean all of them need to *do* anything about it. I just happen to believe in sharing everything and letting the people you are sharing with decide if they need to do something.

(4) Once a month, hold a coaching conversation with each member of your senior-management team. I don't believe in annual performance appraisals. They were invented to give human-resources people something to do and let managers avoid confronting issues with their subordinates.

These monthly coaching conversations give my team members and me the opportunity to raise small issues or concerns with each other—before they get to be big issues and concerns. They also give me an opportunity to coach my managers in a nonthreatening environment on how I think they can improve their performance.

These coaching sessions are just that— coaching. The meeting is a two-way street. Both sides feel free to bring up whatever is on their mind. Believe it or not, this little-done practice builds strong relationships, and both sides really enjoy the conversations.

(5) Have a strict policy of no-blame postmortems of every initiative. You should do this whether the initiative was a wild success or a horrible failure. Everything can be improved. If it was a failure, ensure that blame stays out of the analysis. This is a learning experience and should be treated like one.

Take a lesson from winning football teams. They extensively critique every game, win or lose. You should do the same thing.

Chapter 10

Burnarounds
Choose Their Own Culture

Did you choose the culture in your company?
Or did you inherit one? Are you building a culture of your design, or is it a leftover culture?

To build a culture of your own choosing, start by modeling the ideal employee. What is your ideal employee? I know clearly what my image of the ideal employee is, and I can define it in one sentence:

He/She is creative, committed, passionate, ethical and high-energy, with a high sense of urgency. Isn't this the kind of employee you want in your company? What do you think would happen to your business if *all* your employees fit that description?

> My ideal employee is a creative, committed, passionate, ethical, high- energy person with a high sense of urgency.

A culture is simply a collection of employees. I know you have read much more complex descriptions of culture, and I'm not saying those are wrong. I'm only saying that, at its most actionable, basic level, a culture is its people. So why wouldn't you build your ideal culture by modeling your ideal employee?

The critical part of building your new culture is to put the programs in place that focus on recruiting and motivating your ideal employee. That sounds simple, but is a bit more complex in practice. But it can be done. I have done it dozens of times.

Let's say you want to change the culture to move from management-directed to self-directed. First, you define the ideal employee to work in that environment.

Once you define the ideal employee, put together a multiyear plan to get there. This kind of change will often require turning over most of your workforce. Therefore, you need recruiting programs in place to support hiring the right type of employee. In addition, your current compensation plan might need to be changed to support the new type of employee. I usually replace the typical "pay for how long you've been here" with a "pay for reaching the best of the best" program to support an environment of excellence.

For instance, most vacation plans are based on how long you've been around. If you want a culture of excellence, as in the case of a self-directed workforce, you need to change this so that the "best of the best" people get more vacation than those who have not achieved that designation.

After you have defined the ideal employee, it's time to assess your current employees to see how they measure up. Many won't make the cut. You need to put a plan in place to replace them.

In the meantime, recruit a cadre of ideal people. Now is the time to run a little fat with a few more people than you need so you can continue to operate the business as you are phasing in the new culture. This has to be a rigorous recruiting process that includes peer interviewing by the people they would work with. Once you have a culture of your choosing, the worst thing you can do is bring on new employees who don't fit in. They would work to destroy your new culture.

You need to give current employees reasonable training and coaching in the new way but, if they don't measure up in short order, you need to ask them to leave.

Give the new employees extensive training on the company values and culture. It is the responsibility (with management oversight) of the employees themselves to integrate the new people into the culture.

> After you have all the right people in place, implement self-directed work teams.

After you have all the right people in place, the next step is to implement self-directed work teams. And I do mean self-directed. These teams should get to the point where they order their own raw material, schedule the workflow, and conduct peer performance appraisals. Or, for office teams, planning and directing their responsibilities with little managerial involvement. Sounds like the inmates running the asylum, huh?

Within three years of fully implementing a new culture and self-directed work teams, your productivity should improve 40-50%. At least, that has been my experience. If that's insane, give me more of it.

Keep this in mind: After you design your culture, you have to be sure that *every* process, procedure and policy supports it. You can't have some that do and some that don't. Your compensation plan has to support it. Your communications must support it. Your recruiting has to support it. You have to have leaders that believe in it and support it.

Chapter 11

Burnarounds Hire Only Superstars

You absolutely must have only one class of employees: superstars. Most experts will tell you that this is not possible. They will tell you that every company must have employees distributed along the bell-shaped curve. I simply do not believe this. I have been very successful in populating my companies with the "best of the best." It's not easy, but it is achievable.

A superstar team starts with recruiting. It is damned hard to recruit the best of the best. First, they are difficult to find. They are so good that they don't need to *look* for a job. What tends to happen when companies can't find su-

> If you surround your team with excellence, the whole company will gravitate toward excellence.

perstars is that they give up and settle for someone who is adequate. But adequate will not take your company to new heights. Adequate will cause your company to be just like all the other mediocre companies in the world.

If you surround your team with excellence, the whole company will gravitate toward excellence. That's why you must set your standards ultra-high and insist that people meet them.

Spend a lot of money and time on your recruiting process. My practice is to hire people slower and fire them faster than anyone else. I use a rigorous recruiting process that takes months and months to complete. Even mid-level people are required to go through a psychological assessment and many screenings.

If anyone on the recruiting team doesn't believe the person is spectacular, don't hire them. Use peer interviewing, even in the factory. Remember that you have a certain culture (that should be by design, not accident), and you want to make sure this person fits in.

> **Hire slower and fire faster.**

Notice I used the word *spectacular*. If I'm not really excited about someone, I don't hire them. My hires have to be a "perfect fit" or they don't make the cut. It's a lot easier to hire the right than to fire the wrong. Not only is firing expensive, but the damage that person will do in your organization while they are there is irreparable.

Hire slower and fire faster. How fast?

👀 **Example:** I once spent an entire year searching for a sales manager. I rejected scores of candidates after interviewing them. We put five or six of them through psychological evaluations, yet they still did not make the cut. The recruiting firms hated to do business with us because we were too picky.

Yet, after a year, we finally found the right man. He passed every screening and aced the psychological evaluation. We hired him. And I fired him two months later.

We began to see disturbing signs that maybe he wasn't all we believed he was. His interpersonal skills were a bit on the irritating side (maybe a bit *more* than a bit). He would say inappropriate things at inappropriate times.

You might be thinking that those aren't good reasons to fire someone. They sure are, especially when that someone is your face to the customer. A loose screw can turn business away that you might never even know about. And don't think you can overhaul someone's basic personality — you can't.

As a postscript, shortly after we fired this person, we heard from several of his customers. They told us they were glad we got rid of him because he was "obnoxious" and they preferred not to talk to him at all. Great traits for a salesperson, huh?

And speaking of salespeople, let me tell you the process I use to hire one. Once you get

95

to the point in the recruiting process when you are ready to make an offer, put them to work before you put them to work.

Tell them to develop a 3-year sales plan with as much specificity as possible (they won't know that very much about your company) that financially justifies hiring them. After all, you don't hire salespeople to handhold the customers, do you? Of course not. You hire them to bring in more revenue. So why would you hire someone if you weren't lock solid confident they were going to do this?

Have them sign a confidentiality agreement and give them enough information to do this (without giving away the store to someone you may not hire). I usually find that I can give them a dollar figure for our average content on where our product is used and they can make reasonable estimates from there.

Here is the really important part. Tell them to be very careful and conservative in this exercise because not only will you use it as a basis for hiring (if the number is too low, you won't hire them), but it will become their first 3-year sales goals if you hire them.

Accountability is not accountability without consequences. You need to make it clear that, if they don't come somewhat close to making the sales goals they submit in a reasonable amount of time, you will ask them to leave the company. Let me tell you, that gets their attention.

Keep in mind that this is an imperfect exer-

cise because the candidate can't know everything they need to know to be precise. So you
have to allow for that. And if you think the
plan is not realistic, you wouldn't want to hire
the person just to take them out a year later. So
you have to mix a lot of judgment and fairness.
But it's a terrific process for achieving more
confidence in your sales hiring process. And it
weeds out the ones with lots of fluff and no
stuff.

👀 **Example:** Of the last three salespeople
we were ready to hire, two submitted plans
that they tracked very well with after they
came on board. The third guy never submitted
a plan at all. That tells you something right
there. He either had no basis for claims he
made about boosting our sales (all salespeople
make those claims) or he got scared off by the
"you won't be here if you don't hit the mark"
conversation.

Chapter 12

Burnarounds Establish Values, Recognition and Celebrations

It should be clear to you by now that I pay a lot of attention to the people side of the business. Few things are more important than establishing values, recognizing people when they show them, and celebrating wins.

Frankly, I don't believe in mission statements. A mission statement is usually crafted by people who have no idea what the mission is. They just write something that sounds good and then move on to the next writing assignment. At the end of the day, every company's

> A mission statement is usually crafted by people who have no idea what the mission is.

mission is, or should be, increasing profit and shareholder value. It's that simple.

Values are a different story. Values might sound like a lot of mush, because many businesses establish ones that have no basis in reality. They tend to be platitudes about how a company *aspires* to be. Before the ink is dry, the company ignores or forgets them. And employees know it.

In my view, values are an integral part of a *Burnaround* company. You discover values, you don't create them. Once you have your culture established, you will recognize the values that were naturally created because of a culture by design. You simply codify them and be certain they become guiding beacons ingrained in your culture.

However, you must reinforce these values at every opportunity. Whenever someone in your company demonstrates one of your values, or does so on a continuous basis, make a big deal out of it. Celebrate it. Promote and advertise it. Be sure that everyone knows these values are more than statements—they are the core of your company.

Give awards to employees who show your core values.

Give awards to employees who show your core values. This should not be an easy award to get. Someone really has to walk the talk to get this award. Employees should make the nomination, with oversight by the senior-management team.

Recognize people who receive a values award in an all-employee meeting. Put their face and name on a plaque in your lobby. Take out a half-page ad in the local newspaper so the whole town knows. Nothing beats having your friends and neighbors see your picture in the newspaper. Talk about motivation! Imagine your employees bragging to their neighbors about their company instead of complaining about it.

This sort of public recognition also supports your recruiting efforts. When people see this, they want to know how they can work for such a terrific company.

Oh, and I almost forgot: Nothing beats cash either. Give your values-award recipients a crisp $100 bill.

But be sure you don't let this program become an award "for being here" or "for being a nice person whom everyone likes." This award has to be based on hard, quantifiable, repeatable evidence that this person lives one or more of your company's values every day. Don't delegate this to your "health and happiness" department. You must personally make the final decision and present the award. If this program ever degenerates to a feel-good, without any business benefit, program, fix it or put a bullet in it.

And, finally, a word about celebrations. Look for any reason to celebrate. Celebrate breaking a sales record — with the whole company, not just Sales. Celebrate achieving a significant milestone in a software project. Celebrate a great year. Celebrate just about anything you can think of. The bigger the achievement, the bigger the celebration. Be creative when you celebrate, because that will create a more lasting impression than a ho-hum speech. And when you celebrate, name names. Recognize as many individuals as you can as part of the celebration.

How about a hot-air balloon ride to celebrate a win? Remember my knockout awards (Page 38)? One time, we sent the recipient and her spouse on week long, all-expense-paid scenic train ride through the Canadian Rockies.

Here's something else I've done several times with great success. Get a photographer to take a picture of everyone in your company, but don't tell anyone why. Then have the photos put in a video collage set to music specifically written about whatever your celebration or theme is. Then surprise everyone with it in a company meeting. You can't believe the reaction you will get from people seeing their own faces in a video. At the end of the meeting, give everyone a personalized copy of the DVD to take home. Remember, celebrate with flair!

Chapter 13

Burnarounds Align Every Employee with Profit

This is the last chapter in the book for a reason. If you haven't created a world-class culture of 110% superstar teams, aligning everyone with profit won't work—it will only cost money. Remember, *Burnaround* companies understand two main truths: (1) The job of Team 1 is to increase profit and shareholder value. (2) Your business is about earning real cash money. If you think about that, the answer to how to measure and compensate people becomes very clear.

There is only one number that means anything, and everyone must be aligned with it: profit. Every single employee, regardless of title or job should be motivated to achieve the yearly profit budget.

> **Team 1's function is to increase profit and shareholder value.**

I have seen many incentive schemes in my day. Some of them are so darn convoluted and complex that they exceed understanding.

Why? Well, mostly to try to control behavior. You know the types I mean. The salesperson gets x of this, but only if she is above this number, and only if x and x is met. These plans don't want salespeople pushing low-margin products. So they cut those products out of the incentive mix. Yet the salespeople have to service those low-margin products, so what do we do about that? Hmm, let's put in another "if/but/ and" formula.

These plans don't trust the salespeople to make pricing decisions either, so they always have a limiting factor. It's crazy! Trying to use an incentive plan to control behavior is nuts. Your incentive plans should *reward* behavior, not control it. Controlling behavior is the job of leadership, not policies and compensation plans.

Most plans incentivize different functions for different outcomes. The manufacturing manager might be motivated to hit a cost-of-sales number. Does she care more about sales or cost-of-sales? An engineering manager might be prompted to hit new product targets. Does he care about cost-of-sales or new products?

None of these plans work very well. Does your incentive plan increase your profit or decrease it?

The most successful plans I have built reward every employee for hitting the budgeted profit number, and nothing else. People get a competitive base salary, but the incentive is awarded only if the company hits its profit number. That drives a certain behavior in the organization. You don't have to worry about the salespeople pushing low-margin products just to make a sales number. They know that low-margin products won't help the company hit the profit number and they won't get their incentive money.

You don't have to worry about the manufacturing people hitting a cost-of-sales number at the expense of increasing the top line. They have their eye on the profit ball and run their operation with that in mind.

In this kind of plan, employees concern themselves with what they can do to hit the profit number.

👀 **Example:** Here's a great example of the power of the one-number plan. It was mid-December (the company was on a calendar year) and the profit number was in jeopardy. A factory employee said to me, "Boy, I am really worried about our profit this year; we're 6% below budget. I'm trying to think of what I can do to make it. Do you have any ideas?"

I love it. A person from the factory worried about the profit number! If you're a CEO, is this how you want your employees thinking? Of course you do! To make this work, you have to tell people at least once a month where the company stands so they understand what they need to do. If you are in a privately-held company and don't disseminate that number, simply communicate the percent of achievement to the budget by month. The important thing is not to fudge this number or manipulate it. Credibility in the plan is paramount.

Once again, if you haven't developed the Team 1 culture first, this plan won't work. And, even if you have, you might meet resistance when you launch it. "But I can't control sales" is the outcry from everyone but the salesforce. Sales will tell you, "I can't control deliveries or cost of sales." Engineering will say, "I can't control either one of those factors." Ever heard that argument? Me too—more times than I can remember.

Control is an illusion. As the CEO, can you control sales? Can you control cost-of-sales? Of course not. Even though you have the top job, you really can't control anything. You can only influence these functions. You want everyone in the company doing what they can to influence the profit number. No single job or person can control that number. But together, as Team 1, the entire company has an extraordinarily powerful impact on that number. The key is to get everyone flying in formation. There is no better way to do this than incentivizing the whole place on profit.

Summary

So there you have it. You now know why *Burnaround* companies streak past their competition. You now know why the world ekes by with meager profits while *Burnarounds* lavish in double-digit earnings. And you know why many companies are headed for extinction while *Burnarounds* are winning the global business wars.

But knowing is not enough. You have to take action. So where do you start? With you. First, you have to walk the talk you are about to speak to your organization. If you are not already, make yourself into the model employee you should so fervently desire.

Get away from the office for as long as it takes to map out a 3-5 year strategy for changing your company into a Burnaround. When you come back, set the place on fire!

But get the sequence right. People first, process and plans later.

👀 **Example:** I was counseling with a fellow CEO the other day and he wanted to put my "align every employee with profit" plan into place. I asked him about the condition of his senior management team. It was clear that his senior managers were not "Team 1," so I asked him if every single employee was giving 110%. He laughed at that.

So I told him not to waste his money on "Profit 1" until he had 110%ers and "Team 1" in place. He told me he couldn't wait that long because his company was in deep trouble and he had to get something going quickly.

This is where so many CEOs get it wrong. They want to do something quick and dirty. And, in this example, he hopes that putting a new incentive plan in place will fix the problem that people don't care about profit. It won't. If the root problem is in your employees, your senior management, team, or your culture, an incentive plan is not going to fix that. It will only cost money.

Start at the top of your organization and create Team 1, then task that team to create other Team 1s, one team at a time, one organizational layer at a time, until the entire company has been transformed.

Always remember: Don't mark time. Mark history!

LaVergne, TN USA
28 December 2010
210185LV00003B/139/P